Koestler Voices: New Poetry from Prisons, Vol. 3

With a foreword by Jackie Kay
Edited by Martha Sprackland

First published in the UK in 2021 by Koestler Arts,
168A Du Cane Road, London W12 0TX.

ISBN 978-1-9161817-3-1

Design by Polimekanos

Koestler Voices: New Poetry from Prisons

With a foreword by Jackie Kay
Edited by Martha Sprackland

Vol.3

Midnight Hours

The Self in the Mirror

Afterimage

Fine Detail

Locked Up, Locked Down

Introduction

Welcome to our third anthology of poetry produced by people in secure settings, representing entries to the 2020 and 2021 Koestler Awards. This period coincides with two of the most difficult years any of us have experienced, those in lockdown.

It is in times like these that we turn to poets to inspire us. Those represented here know what it means to be confined, and so they share a very special viewpoint. The title of our 2020 exhibition in the windows of Southbank Centre, '*No Lockdown in the Imagination*' – gifted to us by poet Lemn Sissay – rings true in this volume. Our poets reflect on the strangeness of lockdown from their unique perspectives on space and routine, the minutiae of the everyday, family and memory as well as hopes and dreams.

We thank our poets who have written and sent us their poems at this extraordinary time. They will all receive a copy of this anthology, as will all prison libraries. Our thanks to the T. S. Eliot Foundation for their generous support, and to the many kind individuals who responded to our crowdfunding campaign. We could not have produced this without you.

I would like to thank all the Koestler Arts team who have made the Awards possible for the last two years, and in particular Jo Tapp, Mali Clements, Jenni McGowan, Jon Petre, Laura Pattison and Phoebe Dunn for their work in bringing this anthology to fruition. We particularly welcome Martha Sprackland as our new Editor this year and thank her for all her work and insight.

Sally Taylor
Chief Executive

Foreword

The poems in *Koestler Voices* remind me of what poetry
is for – a poem offers the deepest company and solace,
holds up a mirror to a face in the semi-darkness,
sees you through the wee small hours. A man imagines
his lover is on the end of a call, and the conversation
offers consolation, gentleness, acceptance, but the line
is dead, and the poet is having a conversation with
himself, and his past.

The poems in this collection stretch out and draw
deep inspiration from the poets of the past 'by standing
on the shoulders of the greats / like Seamus did, when
he looked back to Yeats'. Poetry in here keeps the
conversation open between the living and the dead,
the misunderstood and the wise, the imprisoned
and the free. When no other words can be spoken,
the poem walks boldly ahead and holds out a helping
hand: 'Instead the words I write speak in tones
my voice never will'. Here's a collection of poetry
that makes you ask deep questions about the world
we live in and what it means to be human.

It is brave to write the words you cannot speak and
brave to let others read them. Coming from the inside,
up and down the country, the poems offer small chinks
of light, shine the torch on vivid memories, show us
what the poets have held dear, remind us that we are all
defined by love and by loss. From sonnets to free verse,
there's a poem in here for everyone, for that special
someone, who is wide awake in the midnight hours.

Jackie Kay

Midnight Hours

The Call

I was in that shadowed, lonely place
(my mind a random wanderer in the night)
then, incredibly, you were there too:

us both
not quite together, but talking,
a phonecall, but next to one another;
we knew each other's voices.

We said what mattered: my sorrys,
your acceptance, your understanding,
the quiet consolation as overwhelming
as the gentleness of it all

until
with sudden, aching dread I knew:
'This is a dream, isn't it?' I said.
The line was dead.

Anonymous

To Be or Not to Be

after William Shakespeare

To be or not to be? A dat a de question.
Me no know if it something good fe tink about in me
    mind, or me fi suffah
slingshots and bullets of bad luck.
(Can you believe de amount a bad luck weh a fallen me?)
Can I put oars to de water to battle de waves?
To tek sleep and mark death –
right now do me wan give up, lie dung and sleep,
to finish de pain inna me heart and me body, wracked
    wid sickness.
Me can' take dis no more. When all tings said and done
dis a weh me woulda crave. To die, to sleep;
because of all dis bad vision weh a gwan inna me head
me a toss and turn inna me sleep. Aye there's the rub,
for inna dis sleep of tragedy me vision may come
weh me a scrub de skin offa me body
must mek we wait. A de respect
that mek dungfall of lang life
for him who show dem batons and scorns of time,
de wrongs of Babylon, de vain man's insult,
de pains of hated love, de law put on hol',
arrogance of dem weh in high places and de rejection
of people dem think below dem.
When all is said and done he coulda just pay off weh
    him owe
wid de ratchet. Who would carry a buncha wood
to groan and watter run offa him body
but dat de dread of sum'in happen after deat'
(like de Bermuda Triangle where nobody

22

ever comes back from) mystifies de spirit
and mek us carry those bad feelings we have?
Dem strange tings me not know about,
mek us all cowards,
your black, shiny, muscular face
become as pale as if you just seen a duppy
and dis business of great heart and time
is like a mighty river gone astray
and lost its course. Kibba yo mouth!
Ophelia? Firefly, inna your prayer,
remember all my sins.

Anonymous

Black Dog

I survey the area,
It appears to be clear.
So I allow myself into that space,
A psychological place.

I hear a rustle in the corner,
I try my best to ignore her,
But she soon comes bounding in,
As I let the black dog win.

Lewis

The Cell Next Door

A bassline shudders through the wall.
Again. And again.
A rare voice, raised on edge,
silence. A defiant response.
It peters out.

A kettle clicks.
The faint shuffling of cards.
Stamps of celebration when
Manchester United score on *Match of the Day*.
A clear tap-tap-tap-tap
on the edge of the sink.

The snoring begins.
The occasional crumple of bedsheets.
The base of the bed creaking and shifting.
And then
footsteps. A light flicking on.
Talking. To himself.
Regret and promises.
Then back to bed.

I wonder
if he, too,
lifts the blanket over his head,
hugging a knotted T-shirt,
and grinding his teeth.

Richard

Sounds I Hear

Random boasting, bullying and abuse,
scratching, banging, screaming,
animal impressions,
keys and chains,
birds,
dogs,
choking code blues,
smashed-up sinks and toilets,
flooding noisy neighbours,
splashing, crying,
laughing,
drones and mobile phones,
loud TVs,
dance music rising inside,
twenty-three and a half hours
for our privileges
to die.

Anonymous

I Have Become Unravelled

after Friedrich Rückert

I have become unravelled from the world
with whom I squandered so much of my life –
       it's been so long now she must think me dead
       and I do not care if she thinks me dead
       because in truth I am dead to the world.

*

I cannot speak about my then-lived life –
       I've found myself alone. I've found a life
       in the forest of my soul where I live dead
       to the tumble-turmoil of the teeming world.

*

I live my heaven-rest –
       my world-dead song
       my love
       my life.

Anonymous

Prison-somnia

As I lie here on this rock-hard slab
the cold dark walls come closing in.
I can't remember how it was
before this silent din.

Not hearing soulless air vents
with their monotonous droning hum.
Or rainfall bouncing on the roof
sounding out like beating drums.
Mess-filled gutters overflowing
like sprightly waterfalls,
their water drops like hammers
tapping on the walls.

Not hearing taps clonk on and off
gushing through the night.
Or the rush of cisterns filling
as toilets flush before dawn's light.

The buzzing static white noise
of TVs fizzing while most guys sleep.
The footsteps on the landing
as the nightshift gently creep,
with door flaps creaking and torches blinding
they make sure all is well.
Another night deprived of sleep
in this not-so-quiet hell.

I wonder if I'll get used to it?
As days and nights go out and in.
And I try to remember how it was
before this silent din.

Matthew

The Self
in the Mirror

The Wrong Path

I didn't accomplish much
When I was just a kid,
Life under a microscope,
People watching everything I did.

School and me were strangers,
Not a regular place I'd go,
There was nothing it could teach me,
But little did I know.

If sport was every lesson
I'd make the effort every day,
But fortune didn't shine on me,
My young life was mostly grey.

My mum never really knew my deeds,
But I'm sure she had a hunch.
I never learned to read or write,
But I learned to pack a punch.

Before I reached my teenage years
I didn't know my dad –
To learn he lived 5 doors away:
Unbelievable, cruel and sad.

He and I had often spoke
But the truth was kept at bay,
If I'd known of his existence,
My path may have led a different way.

Football was my passion,
My sense of humour often witty,

My skills had caught the eye of
A talent scout for Bradford City.

A different scene to occupy my mind,
You'd think I'd grab the chance with glee,
I'd stopped looking for the fighting,
But it didn't stop looking for me.

Without the excitement of a fight
My life it felt unfilled,
Regular nightmares visit my dreams,
Of the night my 2 friends were killed.

I hold myself responsible,
As I will till life just ends,
They died because of loyalty,
My best, my closest friends.

I went from football to boxing,
I learned to box from very young,
From amateur to professional,
Climbing ladders rung by rung.

Although my life didn't go so well,
I'd had a chance to do what's right,
But lurking round each corner
Would be another flight or fight.

Sent to prison, it was on the cards,
A new life chapter about to start,
My rebellious ways they followed me there,
I broke my nanna's heart.

My sentence not short, it's one for life,
A day bleeds into a week,
Searching for highs to fill my days,
No end in sight, it looks quite bleak.

One thing prison has given me
Is the skills to read and write.
I'll continue on my lonely path,
And I'll beat this thing outright.

Anonymous

Last Train to Lovesville

The stranger's face upon the wall says,
You reap just what you sow,
And the last train to Lovesville
Pulled out years ago,

Rattling across the dusty plains
Of loneliness and sorrow,
Hauling broken dreams toward
Another bleak tomorrow,

Chasing down the sunrise,
Sweeping line of light,
Forever in the shadows,
Always in the night,

Once aboard the juggernaut
That journey never ends,
Rusted rails run arrow straight,
A course that never bends,

Broken bodies line the tracks,
Jumpers to their fates,
For God's divine deliverance,
Or burning through Hell's gates,

There is no driver on this train,
But coal will always burn,
Smoke will always billow
And wheels will always turn,

No carriage will run empty,
No passenger walk free,

There'll be no yellow ribbon tied
Around the old oak tree.

Anonymous

After a Mild Rebuke

It's funny how your criticism stung,
Gently chiding me to do much better,
And, though I smiled, the implication hung,
Long after I had put away your letter.
That day I'd read the speech that Heaney gave
In Stockholm, back in 1995,
His thoughts on poetry were deep and grave,
Reflecting the importance of the Prize.
It's true; I am not fit to tie his laces,
But reading him again re-lit my fire.
We both were schooled in knowing where our place is,
Yet that should not prevent us aiming higher,
By standing on the shoulders of the greats,
Like Seamus did, when he looked back to Yeats.

Stephen

Lego Stings

I swallow my pride; bittersweet
like nickelled apples and barbed wire,
following for your forgiveness.

Our trust is broken,
twelve sharp pieces.
Each fracture made by lovers.

Heart held together by manila paper,
cheap cotton thread, and
ready to burst wet.

I give it willingly to more
than a few. Seeking sweethearts
like a diabetic.

In throes of passion,
laboured breaths
soothe my pain.

Salacious lies lure like Delilah,
to a bed of rosebush thorns,
making masochism worthwhile.

Gripped, set to rip
my skin clean. Blood let
and drip to peace.

Me and you fit like Lego
bricks, but the pain caused
when trodden on stings.

Love is malleable when
ill precedes mal, but I love you still,
when loving bad.

Fights, lies and duplicity lead to more
issues and more heartache.
Tissues heal nothing.

Anonymous

Libation

It was the harbour,
the bright light on the water

(never still,
even now when the tide turns,

the current so slow downstream –
the tide thinking about returning

or the spring flood's force
fast enough to wash one away).

I saw it then:
all the love poured

from my heart into the water;
the vast aching tide of loss,

the things I should have done,
those I can't take back; things

that can never be undone.

It was the river's justice
showed me how,

if I only found the strength
to face the cold dark, it would accept

the offering of myself, my everything,
the whole of me become nothing;

all the good intentions, all the harm over,
poured into the neverending tide.

Is it cowardice or habit
or courage, perhaps,

or my love for you that chooses

moment by moment
to keep breathing?

Anonymous

Look at Me

I get out of a bed that's been shaped by men before me,
I wear the clothes of a thousand men before me.

I eat food I would not choose to eat,
I stand in a shower where thousands have stood.

I walk in a way I no longer recognise,
I am not me I am you,

One of the thousands of men before you,
So I look in the mirror and they all look back at me.

Mark

Current Status

You wouldn't recognise me.
If I were walking down a street you would never
    recognise me
As the girl I used to be
Both physically and mentally.
You would notice everything I carry now,
Though I have always carried it internally
But you never saw it, for it never saw the light of day.
Until now.
Now I bear new scars, new mannerisms, new ways of
    speaking and interacting with people.
Over text I pretend to be my old self,
Though I don't know why.
However in person you would see I have changed
    drastically,
I am a being, to some not human, to others merely
    a passing object.
I no longer speak, I have retreated into my broken shell.
Instead the words I write speak for me in tones
    my voice never will.
The words reveal emotions I have never had
Revealing memories that do not belong to me.
So, please read these words and take them into your
    heart and mind.
Some of these are true and are pleas for help,
Help I have never truly gotten though I have searched.
Please don't judge, just pass along without remark
For this is mine and any person could easily take
    my ability to speak away from me forever.

Katie

Right to Be

I got the right to be me
I got the right to be loud and proud
I got the right to be queer
I got the right to be here
I got the right to be free
I got the right to be seen

I got the right to be vocal
I got the right to be honest and true
I got the right to be confident
I got the right to be here
I got the right to be free
I got the right to be the last of me.

Paul

Beard Haiku

Shaved face
No
More

Scary look
Maybe

But Dad
Don't
Look like
Me

Yorick

The Officer and the Instructor

The officer and the instructor revolve
around each other, handing over
the rehabilitation, or spiritual sustenance
of The Man to each other, every
workday morning. Watchful eyes
chime with welcome consistency –
thank God these two people can
steady the ship, righting a smashed keel
in a channel tempest, her blue steel
scanning the horizon for opportunities
or threats; his permanence steadfast
along the mossy verges and granite,
all as decades-ingrown as him.

People are people and care is care
exchanged as words over lunch
as implied or impassioned, depending
on the overhear; black cotton polonecks
and nylon trousers clink with keys and
chains; men sometimes unpredictable, men
sometimes in pain – the days and weeks pass
with duty in mind, rehabilitated natures
being good to find
when another week and month are done
and the winter turns to spring
the officer and the instructor tend to agree, at least
on the balance that they need to bring.

Sean

In Time

Despite their apparent stoicism,
mountains are broken down
by the persistence of frost.

Against their better judgement,
hills are worn away
by the relentless attentions of rain.

And though they would never admit it,
granite cliffs are ground into handfuls of sand
by the incessant pounding of waves.

A man too may be pulled apart
by the persistence of sadness,
the relentlessness of remorse,
and the incessant pounding of shame.

Yet even as it crumbles,
in time, the earth renews itself
by the slow purpose of tremendous forces.

Perhaps it may be so
for a man in need of redemption,
given time and the tremendous forces
of love and forgiveness.

Anonymous

Shadowkind

Try as I might, I cannot reconcile
This dot that I have become –
'.'
I am small.
A mote that can only catch the light, briefly, fleetingly.
Then forgotten.
Lens.

Do you mind if I survive?

Sunday I woke up on the floor
And try as I might,
My legs failed me.
Some Atlas...

Oh *Jesus Christ!*
I'm getting old.

And the males of my species gathered around,
Sellotaped me back together,
Sticky fingers and animal glue,
Flecks of blood around the nostrils, dead.
(homelessness)

All we are is ingredients,
To be added and processed, homogenised
Carbon, Iron and Water,
Lambs for the Slaughter.
(homelessness)

Over there, in warmer climes:
Doctor said she wouldn't last the night,

Strike me blind, Doc!
(homelessness)

I'm having an Elephant's Time.
My tusks are valuable assets and my species is
    protected,
But I can feel eyes on the Prize.
(homelessness)

My brains is like a detonator, sir,
Best to move on,
Ignore him, he's got people to care for him
(suckerssssszzsssssss)
(homelessness)

So let the Jury deliberate
As to my fate,
I never believed in religion anyway –
(I'm not gullible like you)
As Golem, I was made wrong, and cannot be made
    pious –
(A daft apeth like him, tch!)

Homelessness is hopelessness.

I will be released onto our streets soon.
It's a different dimension, I reckon –
Like the Shaman of Years Past entered,
Portals to Cretinous Habitats.
Dribbled Floors.
I am of the Shadowkind.
Always on the periphery of your vision,
That cool fast runner,
Spring-Heeled Jack.

Across a flat, even landscape.

Your guilt,
You need to take special pills because of me.

Graham

Afterimage

Alone in a Prison Cell

As I sit alone in my prison
Remembering back to bygone days
I cast my mind back to reflect
Saint Patrick's Day when I was free
In a rundown bar on O'Connell Street
Me and my girl supped Guinness
Frothy smiling and moustaches listening
To a band singing 'My Lovely Horse'
Outside the sky electric blue
The sun dazzled bright yellow
People stretched as far as I could see
In the streets singing
No shouting or loud speeches
The people sang one song
Loud and proud over and over again
'You'll Never Walk Alone'

Anonymous

Who Remembers Him?

Staring out my window. Dad did a magic trick
Never came back. Mum handled it
3 sons, 2 jobs, early on the school run
It's only Tuesday. I'm upset because the food's done

I'm from the council estate
All you hear is sirens
A mum's crying
because her son's dying

You got to keep your head up
You got to keep fighting
Because life will knock you down
Like Mike Tyson

Little J wanted to be a barrister
Hyper guy filled up with character
He fell into the wrong crowd
25 years he has to spend in the jailhouse

T was always on badness
T loved a gun
T got shot dead.
Who remembers him?
No one.

Keanu

A Dance for the Heartbroken

God Sylv, where's the salve?
I made a mistake and come to the party late.
All that's left now
Is dried-up pickled onions
And some crusty cheese cubes.

Musty old coots.
But at least I have you.
You turn to me and say, 'No,
No talking now'. You turn and leave
And you go.

So I stay and watch you from across the floor.
Dancing your sullen dance of heartbreak.
I steal a glance through cracked fingers,
Watch a car crash unfolding.

Why did you think it best to leave?
Why did you think it best to go?

Anonymous

Miss that Shit

Sun, rain, cold, sleet, snow, wind in my face...
Taken for granted...
Miss that shit.
Beers out, friends, laughs, pub lunch...
Something as stupid as a cigarette,
Miss that shit.
Moaning mom, moaning son, try, try, try...harder
Nothing ever good enough, it seems...
Miss that shit.
Dog walks, muddy paws, fur babies x2
I'm calling 'Floyd' and 'Irish'...
Miss that shit.
13-hour drives to the Isle of Skye,
Walking Loch Portree with my perfect family...
Miss that shit.
Making merry down Palmers, #UpTheTen
Always finishing with 'dick of the day' @ the Penlu...
Miss that shit.
Being loved, making love, knowing love,
Feeling love, giving love...
Miss that shit.
Door bangs, screams of 'Bitch', window bars,
Bunk beds, locks turn 'til the morning, cycle starts
    over...
Not gonna miss that shit.

Donna

Probably

I wonder what my dad's doin'
right now
he works up in Alaska. and comes home
three times a year. once. to surprise
mama and her boyfriend. and
they are always very surprised
because he always seems
to know exactly where
they are. and
when. once
to surprise me. and he always
brings me a red and black lumberjack
shirt. and once
at Christmas time. when he always
gets drunk and asks me
if I'm still going to be
a rodeo-clown...

      I always say
      probably

Stevie

On Seeing *Christ in the House of His Parents* by Sir John Everett Millais

This workbench; this sawdust-smelling room stacked with
    timber
is like my father's shed: his vice was smaller, but the
    tools hung so, and so –

I would not go there to offer help: my hands were useless;
he was happiest alone, working on some project of
    wood and nail.

This child could be me. This troubled mother could be mine,
head inclined to kiss; to comfort. I can feel her lips:
    wet; cold, to spite her care.

Everyone watches the child: they see something yet to come,
their eyes full of dread; his full of quiet thoughtfulness,

feeling the sting of the nail as it throbs to the tune of
    the heart.
Thus begins the knowing, then: to be here, living;
    to be dying.

Anonymous

You Didn't Come!

A passionate moment between two lovers in
the summertime, we weren't to know in nine
months' time, you wouldn't come.
A visit to the ultrasound suite found you shy,
but we never knew you'd never come.
A nightmare dream, an ambulance in nothingness,
an unearthly warning? We never dreamt you
    didn't come.
A set of trimesters were stressful, was
that the reason you couldn't come?
A normal life turned nightmare, getting close
to when we knew, you hadn't come.
A passed due date, the midwife said, 'this
baby doesn't want to come'.
A heavy splash of blood from mummy's tummy.
Oh you're not going to come.
A swift ambulance ride to the maternity unit,
we had no idea you can't come.
A blade cuts a scar and no baby, parents
in turmoil, this is when we finally knew
you didn't come.

Michael

Boat

Air so fresh.
The biting wind,
the sound of a silent road,
sounds of seagulls will be waiting above
tourists in little shorts with big cameras,
different families waiting patiently
with loaded roof racks.
A stall selling mussels and cockles.
The honk of the ferry
prompts excitement
because I know Grandad would be waiting at the
    other side.
He'll time it as the boat passes his house and meet me
    at the harbour.
Busy, full of tourists, everything in delay.
Waiting for:
supplies,
post,
newspapers.
Little fishing boats with little fishermen
with yellow oilskins –
oversized and overworked.
Speaking Gaelic and racing to sort the fish.
The sense of knowing that you're home again...
that Grandad is waiting with his little weather-flushed
    face.

Michelle

Registration Card 1940

It tells of men in shiny double-breasted suits
And of pipe smoke and fingers stained with ink.
Of women's legs with gravy-browning lines
And fingers tired from typing and mending and death.
It's as silent as the sky before the long low hum
Of planes and the cheerless whistling of bombs.
It lay hidden beneath eighty years of stuff.
Just stuff stuffed in with a load of other stuff
Kept unknown in a box of long-extinct biscuits
At the back of a cupboard in the corner of a room
In the house where my father had lived as a child.
Just a piece of folded card carrying a warning:
'Do not lose', which would have been wasted
On my two-year-old dad. But not on me.

Mark

Statues

Not heroes, they remember the fallible
Who built or did or went or fooled
Once or twice, for something bigger outside,
But failed in private; dug up
By a future generation, an archaeology of sin.

Smash up, remove, destroy, explode
These dribbling plinths of memory:
Wood, brass, stone. Rather, put in every
Congregating place written truths, plaques
Like 'Manners Maketh Us' and 'Do No Harm'.

Something more true than who we are,
That can outlive what's built
In steel, concrete, glass, hubris.
Let me learn to read, look up, live richly
Beyond what generations dispute.

Put up now the broken sword, furnaced
To the caring human form, a helping hand
Devoid of gun or prison key. Plinth instead
Two figures, one resting on a frail another
Yet strong together, more than marble; a gentle love.

Anonymous

Fine Detail

Out There

Through the chilled mist of anaemic rain
I've never been so pleased to see a muddy field.
The season's cycle, masticated rust-coloured earth,
its mud holds captive pools, misshapen mirrors
of passing monochrome sky. In sharp relief,
the evenly spaced line of slender silver birch look
like copper-speckled pale ivory columns. Their

stick fingers seem poised, ready to make music
from Arctic-tinged winds and perform in a
stranded melancholic symphony. Or just, with
subtle sway, conversing with the day. Last
year's abandoned nests stubbornly cling, like
barnacles and limpets, evicted to a leafless
treetop sea. Behind the vacant debris

the circular slow march of turbine blades, silent,
angular, the whiteness belies an ogreish modernity.
Its size dwarfs a gathering of aged muscular
oaks. I wonder... how old are they? Old enough
to have seen emancipation, mechanisation and
walking on the moon. Past autumn's palest
edge, golds reds russets fled the bedraggled

soggy contours of patchy alopecia'd ground.
To catch a brief sight of skittish robin's reddy
blaze, a blatant symbol of chirpy endeavour
among barren stickled branches.
While the thickening swirl of particled mist and
pallid anaemic rain fades my thoughts...
and fades a muddy field to grey.

Anonymous

Love's Herald

Ah, Nightingale, you're honey to my heart,
Almost quite lost with traffic's noisy din;
As nights turn wintry on this windy night
You bring a welcome sleepless fresh fountain.
And Keats, I think on you, now share your joys
Of innocence and beauty never dead,
While hidden owls, hooting in street-lit skies,
Sound omens for the weak and wise of tread.
Ah, Nightingale, you've truly sweetest sound,
For love has blossomed in my heavy breast,
Where future's loneliness has turned around
To future's ocean full of happiness.
          And now that love is lively in the air
          I'll wake bright-early, suffer for her care.

Solomon

I Think They Know

When rivers flow, do they know where they are going?
When flowers bloom, do they know they are growing?
When a bird sings a tune, does it know its own talent?
Do the sun and the moon know they are perfectly
    balanced?
When the rain hits the ground does it know it's nutrition?
When a tree climbs the sky does it know its ambition?
When the stars fill the night do they know we can see?
Does the caterpillar know what it will be?
When the wind flutters by, does it know that it's cool?
Does the pearl in its shell know it's a jewel?
Does the grass in the park know when it's played on?
Does the sand on the beach know where it came from?
When winter turns spring do the bees know the season?
When a baby is born do they know the reason?
I think they know, but I don't know why.
I think the beach knows the sea, and the sea knows
    the sky.
I think the rain knows the flowers, and the flowers
    know the bees.
I think the wind knows the birds, and the birds know
    the trees.
I think the stars know the sun, and the sun knows
    the moon.
I think the caterpillar knows it will be a butterfly soon.
I think nature is a gift, a beautiful show.
The mountains, the trees, the bees and the crow.
Land, sea and sky, sun, rain and snow.
I love Mother Nature, that's one thing *I* know!

Anonymous

Just Beyond the Wire

I hadn't meant to have
a conversation with the flower.
It just happened.
A small, rather ragged foxglove,
stunted, struggling next to the fence.
I felt sorry for it.
After all, Jonah was redeemed
in the eyes of God when he felt
sorry for a withering plant.
Not that I need to be redeemed
by anyone, except myself perhaps.

Talking to plants is a way
to see ahead. You have to
really listen to their replies –
whispers on the vagaries of wind and
a flowing murmur of juices pumping up
from their roots, and their reactions
to the probing of insects.

Listen and you will find answers.

Anonymous

Thing

Today I thought about a thing.
Was it a big thing, a wee thing, a mini thing?
A tiny thing, a minuscule thing? No.
Was it a bad thing, a good thing, a rabid thing?
A nasty thing, a wicked thing? No.
Was it a sad thing, a weak thing, a weird thing?
A joyous thing, a strong thing? No.
It was a thing. Nothing more, nothing less than a thing.

Gilbert

A Precious Habitation

...not that such a man walks and does just as I do,
but because I feel the same spirit and life in him.
— Isaac Penington

At Quaker meeting in the prison
the gulls call words of anger
the bluetit puts together haikus
the woodpigeon gives instructions
and the mimicking clock's tock
mocks my heartbeat.
Outside the room –
the quack of a radio
the thud of laundry dropped
the squeak of tables dragged across the floors –
these all ravel back in the mind's unravelling
and are all assumed into the familiar meeting –
      expected
      useful
      and beloved by us
for noise is stitched to silence.

If silence is noticing
then Quaker silence is noticing in quire.
But no that's not it quite
because the silence does not strain itself
to be one single thing
and because I am allowed
to produce the offering
I produce.

No what I mean is more
that I am made to notice
how the same thing plays differently
on different substances –
letting the pattering song of molecules
be just what it is
to you
as well as me.
It is the action of this particular reach
and stretch of time –

      the pigeon's satirical cooing
      the ambulance sirens.

Yes how the same sitting together in silence
acts differently on the drumheads
of our personal private souls.
Yes how the same light
falls differently on each
of the different leaves of a tree.

Anonymous

Flash Point

Before you coax that match
Aflame
To render solid aspirations
Of alighting upon that mistily promised
Land of perpetual summer,
Shorn of leaded oppression
And caustic blame,
Consider that blunted,
Benign splinter,
With beacon red
Latent potential
For ash and blistering
Winter.

Nicholas

#MeToo

His hands on my skin
Were like sandpaper on satin
And I ache to think
Of all the torn
Destroyed threads

Valerie

Razor Wire

Walking back from gym, the sun,
this late spring evening, lights upon
the coils of razor wire.

And, for a moment, we behold
a blazing filament of gold
that sets the fence on fire.

Stephen

Locked Up,
Locked Down

From 24–3–20 to 6–4–20
(an excerpt)

second day of lockdown
MPs on the radio prose
I cannot call my wife

let out for exercise
but why is the yard so empty
who doesn't need fresh air

today the courting males
are cooing on my window cage
free ~ getting on with life

I search for a bridge shop
but the only one I can see
is on the other bank

today summertime starts
I was taught spring forward ~ fall back
not that I need the sleep

Christopher

Lockdown

In these days of lockdown
This eclipse on our lives
The corona becomes visible
I can hear the birds roaring for territory
They have no fear now for the four-wheeled monster
They, still virulent with life
While we, still boxed in, realise we *are* still nature
The only traffic sound is that of *GTA* on consoles
Our paths of desire overgrown wait for us to walk
To stroll, hand in hand, skin to skin
Nature takes a knee, rests, and breathes
Flowers and virus grow with mathematical certainty
No jet trails rip open the sky
This chain of hours, days and weeks
The story of our life unravels in dreams

Anonymous

The Table

Here sits a man in a room.
It is not his room, but it will have to do for now.
The table at which he sits is not his either,
but it is enough.

On the table, maps of the world
which he reads with enthusiasm and nostalgia,
navigating between memories and dreams,
reliving sights, sounds and intentions.

The maps now have been carefully folded away.
On the table, a collection of belongings;
landmarks in the memory of a life
loved and lost.

Sometimes there are books on the table;
some read, some not, some not yet written.
Thrillers, adventures, autobiographies
echoing his past and his future.

In a moment of weakness, the table bears food;
a veritable feast.
He can remember the tastes
and the internal glow of chilled wine.

Of course, none of it is real,
except the table itself and his imagination.
Although this life is real enough,
and it will have to do for now.

Anonymous

12 Books

Have you made any plans to escape?

Are you a law-abiding person?

You are allowed a maximum of 12 books in your cell.

Do not construct homemade shelves or hooks.

You will be given two sheets of paper per week
for letter writing.

The heating is currently off due to residents using
electrical equipment unsafely.

I have not authorised the release of
your A4 pad of paper.

This must be purchased from an
authorised seller.

Your visit has been cancelled as you are not available.

A letter sent to you contained traces of MDMA
and has been destroyed.

Your clothing parcel will not be authorised as you
recently received a pair of socks.

Film4 is no longer available due to safety
concerns regarding content.

This risk assessment is based on factors which
do not change such as your age.

You have already reached the maximum
number of books in your cell.

You will need to hand some in if you wish
to receive more in the future.

Richard

Doomed

There are cracks in her crystal ball,
Scars in the palms of her hands,
Her wishing well has ran dry,
Dry as a desert land,
Her white horse is but a donkey,
Her brave knight has ran away,
She is trapped in a tower,
By an evil power,
And her dragon is there to stay.

Dean

Autumn, Country But County-wide Closure

'Wiltshire's
Witching countryside'
Is clear: I see
Falling bittern and thrush
Who are near.
I see falling raindrops
And hailstones falling.

Austere.
August (country-wise)
And pears: hidden
Fruit trees in wild orchards
Posing. Dear
To the shadowy leaves, frogs
Spawn their young looking

Unclear.
Unclosed gardens
Have their closure.
It's true that somewhere in
Winter's stare
There is less of a tune
For the earth to spring rhythm

In flintier
Flightier days.

Neil

Not Known at this Address

It's going to be a long time,
a long time
till I am home again.

I make the best of this bad dream.

Be silent they say
the world has done enough crying
but I am not the man they think
I am.

It's going to be a long time,
a long time
till I am home again.

Anonymous

On Our Wing

He is trapped, enclosed
in a bleak mindscape
of falling frogs.

A prisoner, he rambles,
gesticulates, raves in the dark,
and fells a guard with
flailing arm.

Six carry him – marched on
a twelve-legged hearse –
held high, still fighting frogs.

He is gone now.

Will this happen to us all?
This uninvited fall into
our own hermetic oblivion,

when our fingers numbly slip
and – letting go –
we lose the end of the string.

Anonymous

Jail Break

I'll not come back to jail
Simply because
There are not enough hours in the day
Not enough days in the year
And not enough years in a lifetime.

Gabriel

What Prison Sounds Like

Prison sounds like the shittest campsite
You ever pitched your tent on by mistake.
Noise pitches like the Hull to Rotterdam ferry
When United are playing Ajax away.
Prison sounds like a kicked door in a bad dream;
The forgotten magician's assistants
Left inside locked wooden crates on darkened stages.
Adidas drumbeats. A Samba rhythm.
Prison sounds like a house without a doorbell;
'D-WING GATE!' 'C-WING STAFF!' 'MEDICATION!'
There are no 'inside voices' when you are inside,
All voices are turned up to eleven.
Prison sounds like the angry drunken man
You'd cross a hundred streets, whole towns, to avoid.
Or it can rumble like all of the music swirled together;
Gangsta rap, death metal, and the nostalgic love songs
That remind you of who isn't here.
Prison sounds like the TV draw for the FA Cup,
The daily 'click-click-click' of pool balls:
'Prisoner E49####... will be away at Oakwood.'
But then, but then...
On other days, prison sounds like nothing at all,
Like the emptiness of distant space.
It sounds like the surprising silence
Of a dropped clock that's forgotten how to tick.
Or it whispers like playing hide and seek as a kid,
Your own breath loud in your ears. Still. Waiting.
And a nagging fear that everyone else went home,
And perhaps you'll never, ever, be found.

Rob

Kindness, Hope and Compassion

Knots in your gut, you're on the sweatbox to hell
Inside the confinements of your temporary cell
No one to talk to, no one to care
Don't even know if anyone's there
Night-time arrivals are always the worst
End of the line and you're dying from thirst
Searches and questions and given a number
Supplied with a plastic plate and a tumbler

Hurried along, wishing you had died
Open the door and shut you inside
Praying the morning will bring some relief
Enough of this now, can't take any more grief

Continual banging, shouting and crying
Officers oblivious and not even trying
Misery surrounds you and seeps into your soul
Programmed to break you, so you'll never feel whole
Archaic laws that decree it's the only way to stop crime
Society believes rehabilitation's achieved by serving
    your time
So-called 'justice' is corrupt because it's all about
    the money
Incarceration a means to fund the land of milk and
    honey
Only hope can save us and our kindness to each other
Never forget we're either a wife, sister, daughter
    or mother

Anonymous

Plum Blossom (unswept)

There shall no evil happen unto thee:
Neither shall any plague come nigh thy dwelling.
– Psalms 91:10

I tell you how these past few April afternoons
the inner courtyard has been anointed
by three hours exactly
of quince-coloured sunlight.

You say
'Point the laptop out the window so I can see.'

The plum tree is in blossom
alb white
and the daffodils run riot
as if they've been coloured in
by a young child
who's lost his little beautiful heart
to yellow only.

All in all I'm fine –
I sit in my kitchen
and watch the people
in the opposite flats
going about their mundane business
in these unusual times.

And quite a few watch back
and now and then we wave
like passengers on passing ferries.

*

Springtime has marched nonchalantly in
past all the checkpoints we set up.
The season has occupied us.
Birdsong amplifies itself
and daisies and dandelions grow
in the city parks
in defiance of our regulations.
Warmth hangs about in the streets
like frogspawn
and laughs at us –
squatting
in our brick and glass containers
serving our indeterminate sentences
like rubbish anchorites.

*

It's said it will be OK
a lot
but of course it may well not be.
And for many elsewhere this is just
another one of many years
of broken parts –
breakages over and over again.

So among the several lessons
this spring is reading us
here's one –
the unswept blossom
and the smiling unthinned daffodils
tell us benignly
that the earth will not negotiate

(cannot negotiate) with us –
that it would exist
quite happily without us.

It would have time and space enough
in fact
to start to lick its wounds –
to start the slow business
of mending itself
in careful quiet.

Anonymous

Koestler Arts

Koestler Arts (charity no.1105759) is the UK's best-known prison arts charity. Since 1962 the charity has inspired people in custody, on community sentences and on probation to transform their lives through the arts. The annual Koestler Awards generate around 7,000 entries across 52 categories including sculpture, film, music, painting, craft and poetry. Professionals in each field volunteer to judge the awards. 2021 judges include Bidisha, Jeremy Deller, Carl Cattermole and Joelle Taylor, and representatives from Synergy Theatre Project. Entrants gain certificates and hand-written feedback, and can win cash awards, apply for mentoring or feature in exhibitions, events and publications.

Koestler Arts have continued to publicly showcase entrants' artwork throughout the pandemic. Recent exhibitions include *My Path*, curated by young people in partnership with Sheffield Youth Justice Service, at Millennium Gallery, Sheffield; *Soul Journey to Truth*, curated by Lady Unchained, at HOME, Manchester; and *The I and the We*, curated by Camille Walala and Sarah Ihler-Meyer, at Southbank Centre, London.

Each year the Koestler Awards inspire over 1,000 poems – making poetry one of the most popular categories. *Koestler Voices* is published biennially to provide a sample of this engaging and unique writing. Koestler Arts is grateful to the selected poets, all those who took part in the 2020 and 2021 Koestler Awards and the people who supported and encouraged them to do so.

Supporters & Acknowledgements

Koestler Voices Vol. 3 would not have been possible without the support of everyone who joined our crowdfunding campaign. Thank you to each person who has helped further amplify the voices of writers in secure settings this year:

Jeffrey Archer, William Askew, Ariane Bankes, Anne Baxter, Ralph Bell, Crispin Best, Julie Bull, Ross Bull, Emma Carroll, Dinah Casson, Angela Clarke, Alison & Simon Clements, Steve Collett, Lyndsay Cooper, Keith Davies, Wendy Dishman, Edward Doegar, Stephanie Donaldson, Andrea Edeleanu, Jill Edge, Bethan Evans, Sarah Forster, Alison Frater, Keiran Goddard, Henry Grunwald OBE QC, Olivia Hanks, Rosemary Harley, Diana Harris, Joan Harris, Melissa Harrison, John Hewitt, John Howkins, Diane & Ray Hughes, Penny Hughes, Sarah Humphreys, Barry Ife, Richard W. Ireland, Julia, Penny J., Ursula Jones, Elaine Kazimierczuk, Jenny Keen, Amy Key, Peter J. King, Basia Korzeniowska, C. Lindsay, Sarah Lucas, Alex MacDonald, Angela Macfarlane, Jane Mackay, Eleanor March, Clare McGowan, Sian Meader, Caro Millington, Sally Minogue, E. Molony, Sandra Monks, Janet Needham, Jenny Oklikah, Penelope Ormerod, Madeline Petrillo, Theo Pigott, Joyce Quarrie, Deb Rindl, John Roberts, Sylvia Roberts, Tim Robertson, Emma Robinson, Adrian Scrope, Patience Seebohm, Rachel Shackleton, David Shipley, Eleanor Smith Communications, Phillip Spencer, Richard Spencer, L. J. Stacey, Stuart Stone, Sally Taylor, Victoria Thorn, Helen Thornton, Julia Upton MBE, Jill van der Knaap, Penelope Vita-Finzi, Renske Visser, Caroline Walker, John Wates, Sue Whitley, Tania Wickham, Jeremy Wikeley, Rob Williams, Meriel Wilmot-Wright, Kerry Wilson, Christine Wong JP, Stella Wood, and all our supporters who have chosen to remain anonymous.

We would also like to say a huge thank you to our writing judges and feedback volunteers for sharing their time and expertise.